SWITZERLAND

by Michèle Dufresne

Pioneer Valley Educational Press, Inc.

Here is Switzerland.

Here is a mountain in Switzerland.

Here is a lake in Switzerland.

Here is a train in Switzerland.

8

Here is a castle in Switzerland.

Here is a house in Switzerland.

Here is Switzerland.

SWITZERLAND

castle

house

lake

mountain

train